TRANSFORMATIONAL LEADERSHIP
WORKBOOK

YOUR COACHING COMPANION TO UNLEASHING YOUR FULL POTENTIAL

DR. JONATHAN K. JEFFERSON

Written By: Dr. Jonathan K. Jefferson
Designed & Edited By: Aaron C. Butler

ISBN: 9781967082827
Library of Congress Control Number: 2025923857

© 2025 Dr. Jonathan K. Jefferson

All rights reserved. This book or any portion thereof may not be reproduced in any form without permission from the copyright holder, except as permitted by U.S. copyright law.

Printed in the United States of America

BookButler Publishing Company
Upper Marlboro, MD 20774
TheBookButler.com

BookButler Publishing Company titles may be purchased in bulk for educational, business, fundraising, or sales promotional use.

For more information, please email: info@thebookbutler.com

THIS WORKBOOK BELONGS TO

Transformation starts when you commit to your own growth.

HOW TO USE THIS WORKBOOK

This workbook is designed to help you put *Transformational Leadership: Unleashing Your Full Potential* into practice.

Each chapter aligns with the main book and includes:

- Reflection & Awareness prompts
- Action Worksheets
- Coaching Applications
- Living on Purpose reflections
- Leadership Progress Checks

Tip: Dedicate one hour each week to reflection and review. Growth happens through rhythm, not rush.

Table of Contents

Leading With Purpose Begins With Awareness

FROM THE BOOK

This section expands on *Transformational Leadership: Unleashing Your Full Potential* — Chapter 1: "Introduction to Transformational Leadership."

In that chapter, Dr. Jonathan K. Jefferson emphasizes that true transformation begins when leaders understand themselves clearly and lead with purpose. It is through reflection that leaders gain clarity about who they are and how they influence others.

Use this section to apply that awareness in practice—define your core values, strengthen daily habits, and craft a leadership promise that reflects both purpose and authenticity.

Transformational leadership grows from clarity and conviction.

Before you can inspire others, you must first understand who you are, what you value, and how those values shape the way you lead each day. When your purpose and practice align, your influence becomes authentic, your decisions more intentional, and your leadership more sustainable.

CHAPTER GOALS

- Clarify your core leadership values.
- Express those values through consistent, visible behaviors.
- Articulate a personal Leadership Promise that reflects how you lead with purpose.

WHEN TO USE

At the beginning of a new role, project, or season of growth—and any time your leadership energy feels misaligned or in need of renewal.

"Leadership transformation begins with self-awareness and intent."
— *Dr. Jonathan K. Jefferson*

REFLECTION & AWARENESS

Transformational leadership begins with self-awareness and alignment. Before you can inspire others, you must first understand who you are, what you value, and how those values shape the way you lead each day. **Use the prompts below to explore how your current habits reflect your values and purpose.**

When have you felt most energized as a leader? What was happening?

_____

_____

_____

_____

_____

When have you felt drained or ineffective? What contributed to that?

_____

_____

_____

_____

What values do you want people to associate with your leadership?

_____

_____

_____

_____

What do you hope to transform—in yourself, your team, or your organization?

_____

_____

_____

_____

_____

Which of your current habits best reflect your leadership philosophy?

_____

_____

_____

_____

_____

How do the people you lead experience your leadership on a daily basis?

_____

_____

_____

_____

_____

ACTION WORKSHEET:
VALUES CLARIFICATION & ALIGNMENT

Use this space to identify the values that guide your leadership and describe how they are reflected in your daily behavior.

VALUE	WHY IT MATTERS TO ME	DAILY BEHAVIOR THAT PROVES IT
Integrity	Builds trust and credibility	I speak truthfully even when it's uncomfortable.

ACTION WORKSHEET:
VALUES IN ACTION

Choose three values you want to strengthen this quarter. What consistent actions could reinforce them?

COACHING APPLICATION:
MY LEADERSHIP PROMISE

LEADERSHIP EXAMPLE: REFRAMING LEADERSHIP AT AN URBAN PUBLIC HEALTH AGENCY

A new deputy commissioner rebuilt trust by creating a one-paragraph Leadership Promise and holding short weekly reflection huddles.

Within nine months, team engagement rose sharply and performance improved.

What to Apply:
- Use this same approach as you write your own Leadership Promise. Keep it brief, visible, and anchored in your values.

Lesson: Consistency builds trust. Small, repeated actions create big cultural shifts.

Write a short promise that names how you intend to lead others—with 3 observable behaviors you will model.

As a transformational leader, I commit to leading with _____, _____, and _____.   My leadership promise is to…

_____

_____

_____

_____

_____

_____

_____

Who will you share this promise with for accountability—a peer, mentor, or team member? _____

LIVING ON PURPOSE
Your leadership style reflects
the life you live.

LIVING ON PURPOSE PROMPT:

Which area of your personal life—Health, Family, Spiritual, Financial, or Career—most affects your leadership energy right now?

What's one simple step you can take this week to bring it into better alignment?

_____

_____

_____

_____

_____

_____

_____

_____

_____

_____

_____

_____

_____

LIVING THE PROMISE:

Transformation begins the moment you move from awareness to intentional action. Write a short declaration, describing how you will "show up" differently as a leader starting today.

My declaration: _____

_____

_____

_____

_____

_____

_____

_____

_____

_____

☑	CHAPTER 1: LEADERSHIP PROGRESS CHECK
☐	I identified my top five values.
☐	I chose three values to strengthen.
☐	I wrote my Leadership Promise.
☐	I shared my plan with a mentor or team member for feedback.

NOTES FROM COACHING CONVERSATIONS
SELF-REFLECTIONS

_____

_____

_____

_____

_____

_____

_____

_____

_____

_____

_____

_____

_____

_____

_____

_____

_____

_____

_____

Understanding and Applying the Four I's

FROM THE BOOK

This section expands on Transformational Leadership: Unleashing Your Full Potential — Chapter 2: "The Four I's of Transformational Leadership."

In that chapter, Dr. Jonathan K. Jefferson explains that the Four I's — Idealized Influence, Inspirational Motivation, Intellectual Stimulation, and Individualized Consideration — form the behavioral foundation of transformational leadership.

Use this section to evaluate how each principle shows up in your leadership and to design actions that strengthen balance across all Four I's.

Transformational leadership is more than a philosophy—it's a practice expressed through behavior.

The Four I's provide the framework for that practice, guiding how leaders influence, inspire, challenge, and support those they lead. This chapter helps you examine how each of the Four I's shows up in your leadership and create a plan to bring them into greater alignment.

CHAPTER GOALS

- Identify and understand the Four I's of Transformational Leadership.
- Assess which "I" you naturally demonstrate and which needs growth.
- Translate the Four I's into daily, observable leadership behaviors.

WHEN TO USE

Use this section when you're developing or realigning team culture, mentoring emerging leaders, or seeking to align your leadership style with your organization's vision.

"Transformational Leadership is rooted in relationships, guided by purpose, and expressed through the Four I's that inspire lasting impact."

— *Dr. Jonathan K. Jefferson*

REFLECTION & AWARENESS

Effective leadership begins with understanding your natural tendencies. The Four I's help you recognize which behaviors you model most and which require intentional focus. **Use the prompts below to reflect on how the Four I's appear in your leadership today.**

Which of the Four I's do you naturally demonstrate in your leadership?

_____

_____

_____

_____

Which "I" is most challenging for you to sustain, and why?

_____

_____

_____

_____

When has your team responded positively to your influence or inspiration?

_____

_____

_____

_____

When have they needed more intellectual challenge or personal attention?

_____

_____

_____

_____

How do your values connect to each of the Four I's?

_____

_____

_____

_____

What might strengthen balance among them in your daily practice?

_____

_____

_____

_____

ACTION WORKSHEET:
THE FOUR I's ASSESSMENT

Use this space to assess how the Four I's show up in your leadership today. Describe how you currently demonstrate each one, note ways to strengthen it, and rate your overall consistency for each area.

Rating Scale:
1–Rarely demonstrates this behavior   5–Consistently demonstrates this behavior

THE FOUR I'S	HOW I DEMONSTRATE IT NOW	HOW I CAN STRENGTHEN IT
Idealized Influence		
Inspirational Motivation		
Intellectual Stimulation		
Individualized Consideration		

Note the "I" that feels most natural for you and underline the one that needs the most attention this quarter. In the next section, you'll create a quarterly action plan to strengthen the "I" you underlined.

ACTION WORKSHEET:
THE FOUR I's IN ACTION

Based on your self-assessment, focus on the "I" you underlined as needing the most growth this quarter. Use this space to design one actionable activity that will strengthen that area.

Your Focus 'I'

_____

Quarterly Goal | Activity

_____

_____

_____

How I Will Track Progress

_____

_____

_____

Target Completion Date:

_____

What outcome would show you've made progress?

_____

_____

_____

COACHING APPLICATION:
MY FOUR I's PLAN

LEADERSHIP EXAMPLE: INSPIRING CHANGE IN A SCHOOL DISTRICT

A superintendent revitalized teacher engagement by modeling integrity (Idealized Influence), casting vision (Inspirational Motivation), inviting innovation (Intellectual Stimulation), and recognizing individuals (Individualized Consideration).

Within one school year, staff morale and student outcomes showed significant improvement.

What to Apply:
- Use this same approach as you write your own Leadership Promise.
- Keep it brief, visible, and anchored in your values.

 Lesson: Consistency builds trust. Small, repeated actions create big cultural shifts.

In the previous example, you saw how practicing all Four I's in concert can transform a team's culture and performance. **Now it's your turn to put those principles into motion.**

Building on the "I" you chose to strengthen this quarter, use the next page to create a 30-day plan that brings balance across all four—turning awareness into consistent, measurable practice.

Who will you share this promise with for accountability—a peer, mentor, or team member? _____

 COACH'S TIP

Share your Four I's Plan with a mentor or peer coach.

Ask them to observe which behaviors they notice most and where they see your growth.

THE FOUR I'S	ACTION I WILL TAKE	HOW I WILL MEASURE IMPACT
Idealized Influence		
Inspirational Motivation		
Intellectual Stimulation		
Individualized Consideration		

COACH'S CHALLENGE

Choose one action from your Four I's Plan that you can complete within the next 48 hours.

Small wins build momentum—start now and document the impact you see.

LIVING ON PURPOSE
Your leadership influence grows
when you live your values
consistently.

LIVING ON PURPOSE PROMPT:

Which of the Four I's aligns most closely with your personal purpose outside of work?

How might strengthening that quality improve your relationships or community impact?

_____

_____

_____

_____

_____

_____

_____

_____

_____

_____

_____

_____

_____

_____

LIVING THE PROMISE:

Transformation continues as awareness becomes intention. Write a short statement that describes how you will demonstrate the Four I's in your leadership this month.

My declaration: _____

_____

_____

_____

_____

_____

_____

_____

_____

_____

_____

☑ **CHAPTER 2: LEADERSHIP PROGRESS CHECK**

☐	I evaluated my leadership across the Four I's and identified one area to strengthen this quarter.
☐	I designed a quarterly action to improve that "I" and practiced it consistently.
☐	I created a 30-day plan that balances all Four I's through measurable daily behaviors.
☐	I shared my plan with a mentor or team member for feedback.

NOTES FROM COACHING CONVERSATIONS
SELF-REFLECTIONS

Applying the G.R.O.W. Model for Transformational Conversations

FROM THE BOOK

This section expands on Transformational Leadership: Unleashing Your Full Potential —
Chapter 3: "Leadership Coaching for Executives."

In that chapter, Dr. Jonathan K. Jefferson explores how effective leaders create growth through intentional coaching. Rather than simply directing, executive leaders empower others by asking better questions, cultivating self-awareness, and inspiring accountability.

Use this section to strengthen your coaching mindset and apply practical tools for developing those you lead.

Transformational leadership reaches its highest impact when it multiplies itself through others.

Coaching provides the framework for that transformation—it shifts the leader's focus from control to collaboration, from answers to inquiry, and from performance management to people development.

CHAPTER GOALS

- Recognize the role of coaching in transformational leadership.
- Practice key coaching behaviors that build trust and accountability.
- Develop a personal coaching framework to guide your conversations with others.

WHEN TO USE

Use this section when you're preparing for feedback sessions, mentoring emerging leaders, or seeking to shift from managing outcomes to developing people.

"Coaching is not about giving answers—it's about unlocking potential."
— *Dr. Jonathan K. Jefferson*

REFLECTION & AWARENESS

Great coaching begins with great self-awareness. Before you can help others identify their goals and obstacles, you must first recognize your own patterns in listening, questioning, and guiding conversations. **Use the prompts below to reflect on how you approach coaching interactions and where you can grow as a leader-coach.**

When you're in leadership conversations, do you tend to give answers or ask questions first?

_____

_____

_____

_____

How do you create space for others to think and solve problems independently?

_____

_____

_____

_____

What habits help you stay fully present when listening to your team?

_____

_____

_____

_____

Think of a time when your feedback inspired real growth. What made that conversation effective?

_____

_____

_____

_____

_____

How do you currently measure success in your coaching relationships or mentoring efforts?

_____

_____

_____

_____

_____

What might shift if your focus moved from directing performance to developing potential?

_____

_____

_____

_____

_____

ACTION WORKSHEET:
APPLYING THE G.R.O.W. MODEL

Coaching works best when conversations follow a clear process. The G.R.O.W. Model provides a simple structure that helps leaders guide others from goal-setting to action.

Use this worksheet to practice applying the model in your leadership conversations.

STEP	GUIDING QUESTION	EXAMPLE	HOW WILL I APPLY THIS STEP
G **GOAL**	What do you want to achieve?	"What outcome would make this a success for you?"	
R **REALITY**	What is happening right now?	"What's working well, and what's getting in your way?"	
O **OPTIONS**	What could you do?	"What are three possible ways to move forward?"	
W **WILL**	What will you do?	"What's your next step, and when will you take it?"	

Reflect on a recent coaching or feedback conversation. Note which step in the G.R.O.W. process felt most natural for you, and which felt most challenging.

ACTION WORKSHEET:
G.R.O.W. IN ACTION

Now that you understand each step of the G.R.O.W. Model, choose one real coaching conversation to apply it. Use the space below to prepare and record how you guided the individual from setting a goal to committing to action.

G - GOAL — What was the person's goal? How did you help them clarify it?

_____

_____

_____

R - REALITY — What did you learn about their barriers, or strengths?

_____

_____

_____

O - OPTIONS — What possible paths or ideas did you explore together?

_____

_____

_____

W - WILL — What specific action did they commit to taking, and by when?

_____

_____

_____

COACHING APPLICATION:
MY G.R.O.W. COACHING PLAN

LEADERSHIP EXAMPLE: TRANSFORMING TEAM PERFORMANCE THROUGH COACHING CONVERSATIONS

A senior operations executive noticed recurring performance issues across multiple departments. Instead of issuing directives, she decided to approach each conversation through the G.R.O.W. framework.

During one-on-one meetings, she asked goal-oriented questions, invited reflection on barriers, explored multiple options, and ended each session with clear commitments.

Within two months, her teams reported stronger communication, higher accountability, and a noticeable shift in morale. Employees began using the same questioning approach with one another — creating a coaching culture where feedback felt empowering rather than corrective.

What to Apply:
- Use the G.R.O.W. model to guide performance conversations, not just corrective feedback.
- Ask more questions than you answer — coaching begins with curiosity.

 Lesson: Coaching transforms leadership impact when it becomes a shared language, not a single skill. When you model the G.R.O.W. process consistently, others will begin to adopt it naturally.

Coaching is most powerful when it becomes part of your leadership rhythm.

The G.R.O.W. Model provides structure for meaningful conversations, but transformational coaching goes beyond process—it's a mindset. It's choosing curiosity over control and helping others discover their own solutions.

Use the next page to outline how you will integrate the G.R.O.W. framework into your daily leadership practice so that coaching becomes not just something you do, but how you lead.

MY COACHING VISION

What kind of culture or outcomes do I want to create through coaching?

MY COACHING COMMITMENTS

What habits or routines will keep me consistent? (For example: weekly check-ins, monthly reflection logs, scheduled feedback sessions.)

MY COACHING STRENGTHS

Which steps of the G.R.O.W. Model come most naturally to me, and how can I use them to inspire others?

MY COACHING COMMITMENTS

Which steps or skills will I intentionally strengthen this month?

What support or accountability would help you sustain this coaching mindset?

LIVING ON PURPOSE
Your purpose expands when you help others reach theirs.

LIVING ON PURPOSE PROMPT:

How does coaching connect to your personal purpose and values as a leader?

In what ways can you make growth conversations a regular part of your life and leadership?

_____

_____

_____

_____

_____

_____

_____

_____

_____

_____

_____

_____

_____

LIVING THE PROMISE:

Coaching changes culture one conversation at a time. Write a short statement describing how you will intentionally practice coaching in your leadership this month.

My declaration: _____

_____

_____

_____

_____

_____

_____

_____

_____

_____

_____

✓ **CHAPTER 3: LEADERSHIP PROGRESS CHECK**

☐	I explored my current coaching style and identified patterns in how I listen, question, and guide others.
☐	I practiced applying the G.R.O.W. Model to structure meaningful coaching conversations.
☐	I created a personal blueprint for integrating coaching habits into my daily leadership rhythm.
☐	I strengthened relationships and accountability by leading through coaching instead of control.

NOTES FROM COACHING CONVERSATIONS
SELF-REFLECTIONS

_____

_____

_____

_____

_____

_____

_____

_____

_____

_____

_____

_____

_____

_____

_____

_____

_____

_____

_____

_____

Chapter 4: Team Leadership Coaching

Building Collaboration Through Shared Growth

FROM THE BOOK

In this chapter, Dr. Jonathan K. Jefferson explains how transformational leaders extend coaching beyond one-on-one relationships to empower entire teams. Effective team coaching cultivates trust, alignment, and shared accountability—helping groups transition from cooperation to collaboration.

Use this section to strengthen your ability to coach teams toward collective success and sustainable performance.

Transformational leadership reaches its fullest expression when individuals grow together as one.

Team coaching provides the environment for that transformation—it shifts the leader's focus from developing people in isolation to cultivating shared trust, alignment, and accountability across the group.

When leaders coach teams effectively, they move beyond directing outcomes to facilitating collaboration and collective problem-solving. Over time, this creates a culture where every member contributes their strengths, challenges assumptions, and works toward a shared vision of success.

CHAPTER GOALS

- Understand the difference between individual and team coaching.
- Develop strategies that enhance trust, alignment, and communication.
- Apply coaching principles to improve collaboration and team performance.

WHEN TO USE

Use this section when you're building a new team, strengthening an existing one, or addressing communication and accountability challenges within your group.

"Great teams don't happen by accident—they're built through intentional coaching and shared growth."

— Dr. Jonathan K. Jefferson

REFLECTION & AWARENESS

Effective teams don't grow by chance—they grow through intentional coaching. Before you can coach a group toward shared success, you must understand how your leadership influences the team's trust, communication, and alignment. **Use the prompts below to reflect on how you currently coach your team and where collaboration can improve.**

How do you currently help your team clarify shared goals or priorities?

_____

_____

_____

_____

In what ways do you encourage open dialogue and mutual accountability among team members?

_____

_____

_____

_____

What habits or behaviors strengthen trust within your group?

_____

_____

_____

_____

When has your team experienced a breakthrough because of coaching, feedback, or collaboration?

_____

_____

_____

_____

_____

How do you respond when team conflict or disengagement occurs?

_____

_____

_____

_____

_____

What specific actions could you take to create a more empowered and self-directed team?

_____

_____

_____

_____

_____

ACTION WORKSHEET:
TEAM COACHING ASSESSMENT

Team coaching begins with awareness of group dynamics. Use this worksheet to assess how your team currently functions and how your leadership approach supports collaboration, trust, and accountability.

Rating Scale:
1–Rarely demonstrates this behavior   5–Consistently demonstrates this behavior

COACHING FOCUS	CURRENT REALITY	HOW I CAN STRENGTHEN THIS AREA	SELF-RATING (1–5)
Trust & Psychological Safety			
Shared Purpose & Vision			
Communication & Feedback			
Accountability & Follow-Through			

Look over your ratings and notes. In the next section, you'll focus on one area that will make the greatest difference in your team's performance and growth.

ACTION WORKSHEET:
TEAM COACHING IN ACTION

Based on your assessment, identify one area that will most strengthen your team's collaboration and performance. Use this page to design a practical team coaching activity or process you will implement over the next month.

FOCUS AREA

Which dimension will you focus on this month? Why does it matter most for your team's success?

\
\
\
\
\
\

COACHING APPROACH OR ACTIVITY

Describe the conversation, meeting, or exercise you'll lead to strengthen this area.

\
\
\
\
\
\

DESIRED TEAM OUTCOME

What change in behavior, communication, or results do you want to see?

_____

_____

_____

_____

_____

FOLLOW-UP & SUPPORT PLAN

How will you track progress and sustain improvement over time?

_____

_____

_____

_____

_____

LEADERSHIP INSIGHT

Team coaching is most effective when you pause to notice the change it creates—both in your people and in yourself.

COACHING APPLICATION:
MY TEAM COACHING BLUEPRINT

Leadership Example: Coaching Teams Through Change

When a department at a financial services firm faced a major systems overhaul, tension began to rise. The director noticed frustration building in team meetings—people felt unheard and disconnected from the decision-making process.

Instead of issuing more directives, she applied a coaching approach with her team. She began each meeting by revisiting the shared purpose, encouraged open discussion around challenges, and asked questions that invited ownership:

"What do we control right now?" "How can we support one another through this?"

Gradually, conversations shifted to a focus on collaboration. Within weeks, the group designed its own peer support structure, which helped reduce implementation issues and boost morale.

What to Apply:
- Use the G.R.O.W. model to guide performance conversations, not just corrective feedback.
- Ask more questions than you answer — coaching begins with curiosity.

 Lesson: Team coaching transforms resistance into momentum when leaders replace control with curiosity and trust.

Coaching teams requires more than managing tasks—it means guiding a group toward shared purpose and sustained trust.

The most effective team coaches create space for open dialogue, model accountability, and nurture a culture where feedback flows in every direction.

Use the next page to outline your plan for integrating team coaching principles into your leadership practice and strengthening collaboration across your group.

MY TEAM COACHING VISION

What kind of team culture do I want to build through coaching? What does success look like for us?

MY TEAM COACHING HABITS

What regular actions will I take to keep coaching part of how we work together? (Examples: weekly check-ins, peer reflections, shared wins.)

MY TEAM COACHING STRENGTHS

What qualities or approaches help me bring out the best in others? How do they influence team trust and motivation?

MY TEAM COACHING OPPORTUNITIES

Where can I improve my approach to team communication, empowerment, or follow-through?

Great teams grow when leaders listen more, trust more, and celebrate together.

LIVING ON PURPOSE
Your team's growth is a reflection of your willingness to coach with trust and intention.

LIVING ON PURPOSE PROMPT:

How does your approach to coaching influence the culture and confidence of your team?

What practices will help you sustain trust and alignment through every season of change?

_____

_____

_____

_____

_____

_____

_____

_____

_____

_____

_____

_____

_____

LIVING THE PROMISE:

Collaboration grows strongest when coaching becomes a habit. Write a short statement describing how you will intentionally strengthen team connection and trust this month.

My declaration: _____

_____

_____

_____

_____

_____

_____

_____

_____

_____

_____

✓ CHAPTER 4: LEADERSHIP PROGRESS CHECK

☐	I evaluated my team's current level of trust, communication, and alignment.
☐	I identified one area of focus to strengthen collaboration and team accountability.
☐	I designed and implemented a team coaching activity to improve performance and connection.
☐	I established ongoing habits that make coaching and feedback part of how our team operates.

NOTES FROM COACHING CONVERSATIONS
SELF-REFLECTIONS

Empowering Voices and Advancing Equity Through Transformational Leadership

FROM THE BOOK

This section expands on Transformational Leadership: Unleashing Your Full Potential — Chapter 5: "Women in Leadership Coaching."

In this chapter, Dr. Jonathan K. Jefferson highlights the importance of coaching women leaders as a cornerstone of organizational transformation. He explores how empowerment, inclusion, and visibility create pathways for women to lead authentically and make a meaningful impact. By recognizing systemic barriers and amplifying diverse voices, leaders can unlock new dimensions of innovation and collaboration.

Use this section to strengthen your understanding of gender-inclusive coaching and to create environments where every leader can thrive.

Transformational leadership reaches its most equitable form when every voice has room to be heard.

Coaching women in leadership requires intentional support—it shifts the leader's focus from representation to empowerment, from mentoring individuals to transforming systems, and from access to sustained advancement.

When leaders champion inclusion through coaching, they redefine what leadership looks like and widen the path for those who follow

CHAPTER GOALS

- Understand the role of coaching in advancing women's leadership.
- Recognize barriers that hinder equity and inclusion within organizations.
- Develop strategies to mentor, sponsor, and empower emerging women leaders.

WHEN TO USE

Use this section when building diverse leadership pipelines, mentoring emerging women professionals, or creating organizational programs that support equitable advancement.

"When we coach women to lead authentically, we don't just strengthen one voice—we transform the whole conversation."

— Dr. Jonathan K. Jefferson

REFLECTION & AWARENESS

Coaching women in leadership begins with awareness of the systems, beliefs, and opportunities that shape their experiences. Before you can effectively coach or support women leaders, you must examine your own assumptions and recognize how empowerment begins with inclusion. **Use the prompts below to reflect on your approach to mentoring, representation, and equity in leadership.**

How do you identify and support women with leadership potential on your team or in your organization?

_____

_____

_____

_____

_____

_____

What barriers—structural or cultural—might limit women's growth opportunities where you lead?

_____

_____

_____

_____

_____

_____

How does your coaching style create space for authenticity and psychological safety?

_____

_____

_____

_____

_____

Who has modeled inclusive leadership for you, and how did their example shape your own approach?

_____

_____

_____

_____

_____

What intentional actions can you take to expand opportunity and visibility for women leaders in your sphere of influence?

_____

_____

_____

_____

_____

ACTION WORKSHEET:
INCLUSIVE COACHING ASSESSMENT

Inclusive coaching begins with self-awareness. Use this worksheet to evaluate how your current coaching practices support the growth and advancement of women leaders. Reflect honestly on where your influence creates opportunity—and where intentional change can make a greater impact.

Rating Scale:
1–Rarely demonstrates this behavior   5–Consistently demonstrates this behavior

COACHING FOCUS	CURRENT REALITY	HOW I CAN STRENGTHEN THIS AREA	SELF-RATING (1–5)
Representation & Visibility			
Mentorship & Sponsorship			
Voice & Influence			
Workplace Flexibility & Support			

Review your ratings and notes. In the next section, you'll focus on one area of inclusion you can immediately strengthen through your leadership or coaching approach.

ACTION WORKSHEET:
INCLUSIVE COACHING IN ACTION

Coaching for inclusion means moving from awareness to action. Use this page to design a focused strategy or initiative that supports the growth and visibility of women leaders within your team or organization.

FOCUS AREA

Which area from your assessment will you prioritize for improvement? Why is it critical to your leadership environment?

_____

_____

_____

_____

_____

_____

COACHING STRATEGY OR INITIATIVE

Describe the specific coaching conversation, mentoring effort, or policy change you will implement to strengthen inclusion and empowerment.

_____

_____

_____

_____

_____

_____

INTENDED IMPACT

What change or outcome do you hope to create? How will success look or feel for those involved?

_____

_____

_____

_____

_____

FOLLOW-UP & SUPPORT PLAN

How will you sustain this progress? Who can partner with you to keep the momentum?

_____

_____

_____

_____

_____

LEADERSHIP INSIGHT

Inclusive coaching begins when leaders use their influence to open doors for others.

COACHING APPLICATION:
MY INCLUSIVE COACHING BLUEPRINT

LEADERSHIP EXAMPLE: COACHING WOMEN TOWARD INFLUENCE

A senior executive in a healthcare organization noticed that several high-potential women leaders were hesitant to speak up in cross-departmental meetings. Instead of assigning presentation tasks or offering generic encouragement, she initiated small-group coaching sessions focused on confidence, storytelling, and influence.

During these sessions, she invited participants to identify how their unique perspectives added value to strategic decisions. She also coached senior male leaders to ask more open questions and invite balanced participation.

Over the course of six months, meeting dynamics shifted noticeably — women were presenting, leading project briefings, and influencing organizational strategy with confidence and authenticity.

What to Apply:
- Use coaching to amplify underrepresented voices, not to correct them.
- Create spaces where women can express their leadership in authentic and empowering ways.

 Lesson: Inclusive coaching expands influence when leaders model equity, challenge bias, and open opportunities for every voice to be heard.

Inclusive leadership begins when awareness meets intentional action.

Coaching becomes transformative when it amplifies diverse voices and removes barriers that limit personal and professional growth.

Use the next page to outline how you will integrate inclusive coaching into your leadership—creating pathways for women to lead, influence, and thrive.

COACH'S CHALLENGE

In your next meeting or mentoring session, make space for a woman leader to share an idea or success story. Observe how visibility changes confidence—and how confidence strengthens culture.

MY INCLUSION VISION

What kind of culture or environment do I want to create through my coaching? How will it empower women to lead authentically?

MY COACHING PRACTICES

What consistent actions or habits will I build into my leadership to support inclusion and equity? (Examples: mentoring circles, equitable feedback, visibility opportunities.)

MY STRENGTHS AS AN ALLY OR ADVOCATE

What qualities or experiences help me champion others' growth and confidence?

MY GROWTH OPPORTUNITIES

Where can I improve in recognizing bias, sharing opportunities, or modeling inclusivity?

Real inclusion happens when leaders use their influence
to make room for others at the table.

LIVING ON PURPOSE
Your influence multiplies
when you use your voice to
elevate others.

LIVING ON PURPOSE PROMPT:

How does your leadership coaching contribute to greater equity and visibility for women in your organization or community?

What actions can you take to make inclusion a defining part of your leadership identity?

_____

_____

_____

_____

_____

_____

_____

_____

_____

_____

_____

_____

_____

LIVING THE PROMISE:

Equity grows stronger through consistent action. Write a short statement describing how you will intentionally support, mentor, or advocate for women leaders this month.

My declaration: _____

_____

_____

_____

_____

_____

_____

_____

_____

_____

✓ **CHAPTER 5: LEADERSHIP PROGRESS CHECK**

☐	I examined my own beliefs and habits that influence how I coach and empower women leaders.
☐	I identified structural or cultural barriers that limit inclusion and opportunity.
☐	I designed and implemented an inclusive coaching strategy to strengthen equity and visibility.
☐	I committed to ongoing habits that use my influence to mentor, sponsor, and advocate for women in leadership.

NOTES FROM COACHING CONVERSATIONS
SELF-REFLECTIONS

_____
_____
_____
_____
_____
_____
_____
_____
_____
_____
_____
_____
_____
_____
_____
_____
_____
_____
_____
_____

Leading with Purpose, Stewardship, and Sustainable Impact

FROM THE BOOK

This section expands on Transformational Leadership: Unleashing Your Full Potential — Chapter 6: "Transformational Leadership in Nonprofit Organizations."

In this chapter, Dr. Jonathan K. Jefferson examines how nonprofit leaders can balance mission and management to create lasting community change. He highlights how transformational leadership principles—vision, empowerment, and accountability—help organizations move beyond survival to sustainability.

Use this section to strengthen your ability to lead mission-driven teams with integrity, strategy, and compassion.

Transformational leadership in nonprofit organizations requires striking a balance between vision, stewardship, and compassion.

Unlike in for-profit settings, nonprofit leaders are driven not by competition, but by contribution—mobilizing people and resources toward a shared purpose that outlasts financial cycles or personal recognition.

Nonprofit leaders often face the tension between financial sustainability and fidelity to their mission. True transformational leadership means resisting the pull to chase every funding opportunity and instead ensuring that each partnership, program, or grant directly supports the organization's purpose and values.

This chapter helps you reflect on how your leadership decisions align with your mission and how you can strengthen trust, accountability, and long-term impact in your organization.

CHAPTER GOALS

- Understand the unique challenges and opportunities of nonprofit leadership.
- Strengthen alignment between mission, values, and daily operations.
- Apply transformational practices that balance purpose, stewardship, and sustainable impact.

WHEN TO USE

Use this section when leading mission-driven teams, strengthening organizational alignment, or navigating funding, staffing, or community-impact challenges.

"Mission gives purpose, but leadership gives it life."

— *Dr. Jonathan K. Jefferson*

REFLECTION & AWARENESS

Nonprofit leadership demands both vision and resilience.

Before you can inspire others to serve, you must reflect on how your leadership aligns with the mission, values, and realities of the communities you serve. **Use the prompts below to consider how transformational leadership principles shape your effectiveness in nonprofit environments.**

How do you balance your organization's mission with the practical realities of funding, staffing, and sustainability?

_____

_____

_____

_____

_____

What daily leadership behaviors help you keep your team focused on purpose rather than pressure?

_____

_____

_____

_____

How do you ensure that collaboration, inclusion, and accountability remain central to your organization's culture?

_____

_____

_____

_____

_____

When have you witnessed transformational leadership make a tangible difference in your nonprofit or community setting?

_____

_____

_____

_____

_____

How do you maintain resilience and clarity when challenges threaten your organization's mission or resources?

_____

_____

_____

_____

_____

ACTION WORKSHEET:
MISSION ALIGNMENT ASSESSMENT

Every transformational leader in the nonprofit sector must connect vision to action. Use this worksheet to assess how well your organization's daily practices align with its mission, values, and long-term goals. Reflect honestly to identify both strengths and opportunities for deeper alignment.

Rating Scale:
1–Rarely demonstrates this behavior   5–Consistently demonstrates this behavior

FOCUS AREA	CURRENT REALITY	HOW I CAN STRENGTHEN THIS AREA	SELF-RATING (1–5)
Mission Clarity			
Resource Stewardship			
Team Engagement			
Community Impact			

Review your ratings and notes. In the next section, you'll choose one area of alignment to strengthen and design a focused strategy to bring your mission to life through leadership.

ACTION WORKSHEET:
MISSION ALIGNMENT IN ACTION

Mission alignment happens when what your organization believes is reflected in what it does. Use this page to design one specific initiative or leadership action that strengthens the connection between your mission, strategy, and daily operations.

FOCUS AREA

Which area from your assessment will you strengthen first? Why is it essential to your organization's mission and long-term success?

_____

_____

_____

_____

_____

_____

LEADERSHIP ACTION OR INITIATIVE

Describe the specific step, project, or conversation that will help bring your mission and practices into better alignment.

_____

_____

_____

_____

_____

_____

INTENDED IMPACT

What difference will this action make for your team, your stakeholders, or the community you serve?

_____

_____

_____

_____

_____

SUSTAINABILITY PLAN

How will you ensure this alignment continues? What systems, habits, or checkpoints will help sustain progress?

_____

_____

_____

_____

_____

LEADERSHIP INSIGHT

Purpose-driven organizations thrive when leaders align passion with process.

COACHING APPLICATION:
MY MISSION ALIGNMENT BLUEPRINT

LEADERSHIP EXAMPLE: LEADING WITH PURPOSE AND STEWARDSHIP

A nonprofit director overseeing a youth mentoring organization noticed her team was struggling with burnout and declining engagement. As grant requirements became increasingly complex, staff became focused on compliance instead of community impact.

Recognizing this drift, the director initiated a "Mission Reset" series—monthly coaching sessions where the team reconnected their daily work to the organization's core purpose. Each session began with a story of transformation from the field and ended with a discussion on how every role contributed to long-term outcomes.

Within three months, staff morale improved, retention stabilized, and the team began developing new partnerships rooted in shared mission values rather than funding convenience.

What to Apply:
- Revisit your organization's mission regularly to ensure decisions reflect purpose, not pressure.
- Model stewardship by connecting operational excellence to community impact.

 Lesson: Mission alignment sustains transformation—when leaders stay grounded in purpose, they keep people inspired and programs effective.

Purpose-driven leadership requires discipline, reflection, and intentional alignment.

Transformational leaders in nonprofit organizations don't just manage programs —they steward purpose.

Use this page to outline how you will strengthen alignment between your mission, operations, and leadership practices.

COACH'S CHALLENGE

This week, start one meeting by asking your team to share a story that captures your organization's mission in action. Notice how energy and focus shift when purpose leads the conversation.

MY MISSION COMMITMENT

What aspect of your organization's mission most inspires you? How does it shape the way you lead each day?

MY ALIGNMENT ACTIONS

What practical steps will you take to ensure daily decisions, communications, and partnerships reflect your mission's core values?

MY LEADERSHIP STRENGTHS

What leadership qualities help you model accountability, stewardship, and purpose-driven influence?

MY GROWTH OPPORTUNITIES

Where can you grow to lead with greater balance between passion, strategy, and sustainability?

Mission-driven leadership thrives when passion is guided by purpose and anchored in integrity.

LIVING ON PURPOSE
Your organization's strength grows when purpose guides every decision.

LIVING ON PURPOSE PROMPT:

How does your leadership reflect the mission and values of your organization?

In what ways can you ensure that purpose remains central in both strategy and daily practice?

_____

_____

_____

_____

_____

_____

_____

_____

_____

_____

_____

_____

_____

_____

LIVING THE PROMISE:

Transformation in nonprofit leadership happens when purpose becomes practice. Write a short statement describing how you will strengthen mission alignment in your leadership this month.

My declaration: _____

_____

_____

_____

_____

_____

_____

_____

_____

_____

_____

☑ CHAPTER 6: LEADERSHIP PROGRESS CHECK

☐	I evaluated how my organization's daily operations align with its mission, vision, and values.
☐	I identified key areas where leadership actions can better reflect purpose and stewardship.
☐	I designed and implemented a mission-focused initiative to strengthen alignment and impact.
☐	I committed to ongoing practices that connect team performance to organizational purpose.

NOTES FROM COACHING CONVERSATIONS
SELF-REFLECTIONS

Bridging Generations Through Purpose, Feedback, and Collaboration

FROM THE BOOK

This section expands on Transformational Leadership: Unleashing Your Full Potential — Chapter 7: "Leadership Coaching for Millennials."

In this chapter, Dr. Jonathan K. Jefferson explores how transformational leaders can effectively coach and engage millennial professionals. He emphasizes the importance of authenticity, purpose, and continuous feedback in motivating this generation to lead with creativity and collaboration. By understanding their values —connection, flexibility, and impact—leaders can create environments where innovation thrives and engagement deepens.

Use this section to refine how you communicate, coach, and collaborate across generations to build a culture of mutual respect and shared growth.

Transformational leadership adapts to the needs and strengths of each generation.

Coaching millennials requires leaders to shift from hierarchy to partnership, from authority to authenticity, and from performance oversight to developmental dialogue. When leaders embrace transparency, purpose, and feedback as core coaching tools, they build trust and unlock potential in emerging leaders.

The result is a culture where purpose drives performance and collaboration fuels innovation.

CHAPTER GOALS

- Understand generational differences in leadership motivation and engagement.
- Develop coaching approaches that foster autonomy, purpose, and trust among millennials.
- Strengthen communication and feedback practices to sustain collaboration and innovation.

WHEN TO USE

Use this section when mentoring emerging professionals, leading cross-generational teams, or developing leadership pipelines that prioritize purpose and partnership.

"Millennial leaders don't just want to work for organizations—they want to work with them to make a difference."

— *Dr. Jonathan K. Jefferson*

REFLECTION & AWARENESS

Coaching millennials begins with understanding what drives them. Before you can effectively lead emerging professionals, you must reflect on how your leadership style fosters trust, communication, and shared purpose. **Use the prompts below to explore how you engage, develop, and empower millennial leaders in your organization.**

How do you currently connect organizational goals to the sense of purpose millennials seek in their work?

_____

_____

_____

_____

_____

_____

What habits or behaviors help you provide meaningful feedback and recognition consistently?

_____

_____

_____

_____

_____

_____

How do you balance structure with flexibility to keep your team motivated and engaged?

_____

_____

_____

_____

_____

When have you learned something valuable by listening to or collaborating with a millennial colleague?

_____

_____

_____

_____

_____

What specific actions can you take to build trust and empower millennial leaders to grow within your organization?

_____

_____

_____

_____

_____

ACTION WORKSHEET:
GENERATIONAL COACHING ASSESSMENT

Coaching across generations requires awareness, adaptability, and intentional communication. Use this worksheet to assess how effectively you engage, motivate, and develop millennial leaders. Reflect honestly on your current practices to identify where greater connection, flexibility, or feedback could strengthen results.

Rating Scale:
1–Rarely demonstrates this behavior   5–Consistently demonstrates this behavior

COACHING FOCUS	CURRENT REALITY	HOW I CAN STRENGTHEN THIS AREA	SELF-RATING (1–5)
Purpose Alignment			
Feedback & Communication			
Flexibility & Autonomy			
Collaboration & Inclusion			

Review your ratings and notes. In the next section, you'll choose one area of focus to strengthen your connection and coaching effectiveness with millennial leaders.

ACTION WORKSHEET:
GENERATIONAL COACHING IN ACTION

Coaching millennials effectively means transforming awareness into meaningful action. Use this page to design one focused coaching strategy that strengthens connection, motivation, and engagement among emerging leaders on your team.

FOCUS AREA

Which coaching area from your assessment needs the most attention? Why is this important for your team's growth and engagement?

_____

_____

_____

_____

_____

_____

COACHING STRATEGY OF ACTION STEP

Describe one specific way you will adjust your communication, feedback, or leadership approach to better support millennial leaders.

_____

_____

_____

_____

_____

_____

EXPECTED OUTCOME

What change in motivation, collaboration, or performance do you expect to see as a result?

_____

_____

_____

_____

_____

FOLLOW-UP PLAN

How will you measure progress and maintain consistency in your approach?

_____

_____

_____

_____

_____

LEADERSHIP INSIGHT

Coaching across generations builds bridges of understanding that turn shared purpose into lasting impact.

COACHING APPLICATION:
MY GENERATIONAL COACHING BLUEPRINT

LEADERSHIP EXAMPLE: COACHING ACROSS GENERATIONS

A senior manager at a technology firm was struggling to keep a multigenerational team aligned. His veteran staff preferred structure and predictability, while his millennial team members wanted flexibility and a voice in decisions. Tension was rising, and productivity was slipping.

Instead of enforcing tighter rules, he decided to experiment with coaching conversations. He invited the team to share how they preferred to receive feedback and what helped them stay motivated. The group agreed to replace traditional status updates with short "pulse check" meetings where everyone could raise challenges and share quick wins.

Within two months, collaboration improved, turnover risk decreased, and the team began mentoring one another—bridging generational divides through shared purpose and transparency.

What to Apply:
- Replace one-way communication with dialogue that values every generation's perspective.
- Encourage shared ownership and collaboration through frequent, intentional check-ins.

 Lesson: Transformational coaching bridges generations when leaders listen with curiosity and lead with authenticity.

Coaching across generations requires intention and adaptability.

Transformational leaders bridge generational differences by creating cultures of trust, feedback, and shared purpose.

Use this page to outline how you will coach, communicate, and collaborate with millennial leaders—and model the inclusive, purpose-driven leadership they value.

 COACH'S TIP

**Every generation values being heard.
Ask questions that reveal what motivates your team,
then listen as if the future of your organization depends
on their answers—it often does.**

MY CONNECTION STRATEGY

How will I strengthen relationships and trust with millennial leaders on my team? What conversations or actions will I initiate?

MY COACHING HABITS

What consistent behaviors will I practice to provide feedback, support growth, and sustain engagement?

MY LEADERSHIP STRENGTHS

Which personal qualities help me relate to and motivate younger generations? How can I use them more intentionally?

MY GROWTH OPPORTUNITIES

Where can I improve in adapting communication, empowering autonomy, or fostering collaboration across generations?

The best leaders don't bridge generations by changing who they are—they bridge them by listening, adapting, and empowering others to lead.

LIVING ON PURPOSE
Your ability to lead generations begins with your willingness to listen, learn, and adapt.

LIVING ON PURPOSE PROMPT:

How does your approach to coaching foster connection and growth among emerging leaders?

What can you do to strengthen trust and collaboration across generational lines?

_____

_____

_____

_____

_____

_____

_____

_____

_____

_____

_____

_____

_____

_____

LIVING THE PROMISE:

> Growth across generations begins with intentional communication and shared purpose. Write a short statement describing how you will strengthen collaboration and connection with millennial leaders this month.

My declaration: _____

_____

_____

_____

_____

_____

_____

_____

_____

_____

☑ CHAPTER 7: LEADERSHIP PROGRESS CHECK

☐	I reflected on how my leadership style supports connection, trust, and engagement across generations.
☐	I identified specific strategies to adapt communication and feedback for millennial leaders.
☐	I implemented one actionable change to strengthen collaboration and shared ownership within my team.
☐	I committed to continuous learning and dialogue that bridges generational perspectives.

NOTES FROM COACHING CONVERSATIONS
SELF-REFLECTIONS

_____

_____

_____

_____

_____

_____

_____

_____

_____

_____

_____

_____

_____

_____

_____

_____

_____

_____

_____

_____

Inspiring Growth, Equity, and Excellence in Learning Communities

FROM THE BOOK

This section expands on Transformational Leadership: Unleashing Your Full Potential — Chapter 8: "Educational Leadership Coaching."

In this chapter, Dr. Jonathan K. Jefferson explores how transformational coaching empowers educators and administrators to create environments where learning, equity, and innovation thrive.
He emphasizes the power of reflective practice, emotional intelligence, and shared accountability in developing both students and staff.

Use this section to examine how your leadership influences school culture, strengthens teacher effectiveness, and models lifelong learning for the next generation.

Transformational leadership in education begins with belief—belief in people, potential, and progress.

Coaching educators requires leaders to move from supervision to partnership, from compliance to collaboration, and from evaluation to empowerment.
When educational leaders focus on growth rather than control, they unlock creativity and foster a stronger collective purpose.

The result is a learning culture where every teacher, student, and stakeholder can flourish.

CHAPTER GOALS

- Understand how transformational coaching principles can be applied in educational settings.
- Strengthen reflective and collaborative practices that empower teachers and staff.
- Develop strategies to foster equitable and innovative learning environments.

WHEN TO USE

Use this section when mentoring teachers, leading academic teams, or implementing schoolwide improvement initiatives that depend on trust, feedback, and shared accountability.

"Educational leadership is not about managing outcomes—it's about inspiring growth."

— Dr. Jonathan K. Jefferson

REFLECTION & AWARENESS

Educational leadership begins with self-awareness and the courage to grow. Before you can inspire learning in others, you must reflect on how your beliefs, actions, and communication shape your school's culture. **Use the prompts below to explore how transformational coaching can strengthen your leadership impact in education.**

How do your daily leadership decisions reflect your belief in the potential of every student and educator?

_____

_____

_____

_____

_____

_____

What practices do you use to model continuous learning and professional growth for your team?

_____

_____

_____

_____

_____

_____

How do you foster collaboration and trust among teachers, staff, and administrators?

_____

_____

_____

_____

_____

How do you balance accountability with empathy when coaching educators through challenges?

_____

_____

_____

_____

_____

What actions can you take to build a school culture rooted in equity, reflection, and shared purpose?

_____

_____

_____

_____

_____

ACTION WORKSHEET:
EDUCATIONAL COACHING ASSESSMENT

Educational coaching strengthens leadership by turning reflection into growth. Use this worksheet to assess how your current practices support collaboration, continuous learning, and equity within your school or educational organization. Reflect honestly on where your leadership builds capacity—and where it can grow stronger.

Rating Scale:
1–Rarely demonstrates this behavior   5–Consistently demonstrates this behavior

COACHING FOCUS	CURRENT REALITY	HOW I CAN STRENGTHEN THIS AREA	SELF-RATING (1–5)
Vision & Alignment			
Collaboration & Trust			
Feedback & Reflection			
Equity & Inclusion			

Review your responses and identify one area of educational coaching that would have the greatest impact if strengthened. You'll use this focus to develop a targeted plan in the next section.

ACTION WORKSHEET:
EDUCATIONAL COACHING IN ACTION

Educational coaching becomes transformational when reflection leads to tangible change. Use this page to design one specific initiative or leadership action that strengthens collaboration, learning, and empowerment across your educational community.

FOCUS AREA

Which area from your assessment will you prioritize for improvement? Why is it vital to your school or team's success?

_____

_____

_____

_____

_____

_____

LEADERSHIP ACTION OR INITIATIVE

Describe the specific step, strategy, or coaching approach you will take to strengthen learning, collaboration, or equity.

_____

_____

_____

_____

_____

_____

INTENDED IMPACT

What measurable or observable outcomes do you expect for educators, students, or your broader learning community?

_____

_____

_____

_____

_____

_____

SUSTAINABILITY PLAN

How will you ensure this progress continues over time? What systems or supports will help maintain momentum?

_____

_____

_____

_____

_____

_____

LEADERSHIP INSIGHT

Coaching educators with purpose turns improvement plans into growth cultures.

COACHING APPLICATION:
MY EDUCATIONAL COACHING BLUEPRINT

LEADERSHIP EXAMPLE: COACHING FOR SCHOOL-WIDE GROWTH

A principal at a mid-sized high school noticed that her staff meetings had become focused on compliance rather than collaboration. Teachers were meeting performance standards, but morale and innovation were declining.

Instead of introducing new mandates, she initiated a series of peer coaching sessions where teachers observed one another's classrooms and shared reflective feedback in a supportive format.

Within a semester, professional dialogue replaced defensiveness. Teachers began experimenting with new strategies, co-creating lesson plans, and celebrating shared successes. The principal reported not only improved instructional quality but also a renewed sense of community and professional pride across the staff.

What to Apply:
- Use coaching to shift the focus from evaluation to growth.
- Create space for collaboration and reflective practice among educators.

 Lesson: Coaching transforms schools when leaders replace compliance with curiosity and empower teachers to lead learning together.

Transformational educational leadership thrives on reflection, empowerment, and shared purpose.

Coaching creates a culture where teachers grow as leaders and students benefit from inspired instruction.

Use this page to define how you will apply transformational coaching principles to strengthen growth, trust, and innovation in your learning environment.

 COACH'S TIP

Growth multiplies when leaders shift from observing to learning alongside their teams.
Be the first to model reflection—it turns feedback into trust.

MY COACHING VISION

What kind of learning culture do I want to create through my coaching and leadership?

MY STRATEGIC ACTIONS

What consistent steps will I take to model reflection, collaboration, and growth across my team or school?

MY LEADERSHIP STRENGTHS

Which personal strengths or experiences help me inspire educators and students toward excellence?

MY AREAS FOR GROWTH

Where can I improve my coaching practice to better support equity, innovation, and sustained learning outcomes?

Educational coaching transforms systems when leaders make
growth a shared pursuit, not a solitary goal.

LIVING ON PURPOSE
Your leadership in education becomes transformational when you coach with vision, empathy, and purpose.

LIVING ON PURPOSE PROMPT:

How does your coaching approach inspire growth and reflection among teachers or students?

What can you do to strengthen a culture of collaboration and continuous learning in your school or organization?

_____

_____

_____

_____

_____

_____

_____

_____

_____

_____

_____

_____

_____

LIVING THE PROMISE:

Coaching educators is an investment in the future. Write a short statement describing how you will intentionally cultivate growth and empowerment in your educational community this month.

My declaration: _____

_____

_____

_____

_____

_____

_____

_____

_____

_____

_____

☑	CHAPTER 8: LEADERSHIP PROGRESS CHECK
☐	I reflected on how my leadership practices influence growth, collaboration, and equity in my learning community.
☐	I identified one key area where coaching can enhance professional development and instructional excellence.
☐	I implemented a specific coaching strategy that encourages reflection, innovation, and shared accountability.
☐	I committed to sustaining a culture of learning where educators and students grow together.

NOTES FROM COACHING CONVERSATIONS
SELF-REFLECTIONS

Chapter 9: Leadership Development Coaching

Cultivating Growth, Confidence, and Capability in Emerging Leaders

FROM THE BOOK

This section expands on Transformational Leadership: Unleashing Your Full Potential — Chapter 9: "Leadership Development Coaching."

In this chapter, Dr. Jonathan K. Jefferson explains how leadership development coaching equips emerging and established leaders to grow beyond positional authority into authentic influence. He outlines key strategies for building self-awareness, setting measurable goals, and creating environments that enable people to lead from their strengths.

Use this section to evaluate your approach to developing others, empowering leadership potential at every level of your organization.

Transformational leadership multiplies when leaders grow other leaders.

Development coaching shifts focus from managing performance to expanding potential. When leaders invest in growth conversations that clarify purpose, build confidence, and challenge comfort zones, they cultivate teams ready to innovate and sustain success. Leadership development isn't a one-time initiative—it's a continual process of coaching, reflection, and renewal.

CHAPTER GOALS

- Understand how coaching accelerates leadership growth and succession.
- Strengthen your ability to identify and nurture emerging leaders.
- Develop systems and habits that embed coaching into your leadership culture.

WHEN TO USE

Use this section when mentoring new managers, preparing teams for greater responsibility, or building long-term leadership pipelines.

"Educational leadership is not about managing outcomes—it's about inspiring growth."

— *Dr. Jonathan K. Jefferson*

REFLECTION & AWARENESS

Leadership development begins with recognizing potential—in yourself and in others. Before you can coach emerging leaders effectively, you must understand how your habits, communication, and mindset influence their growth. **Use the prompts below to reflect on your role as a developer of people and builder of future leaders.**

How do you identify and nurture leadership potential within your organization or team?

_____

_____

_____

_____

What practices or conversations help you challenge emerging leaders while supporting their confidence?

_____

_____

_____

_____

How do you balance offering guidance with allowing others to take ownership and make decisions?

_____

_____

_____

_____

Who has invested in your own leadership journey, and how has their coaching shaped your approach to developing others?

_____

_____

_____

_____

_____

How do you create a safe environment for feedback, experimentation, and leadership growth?

_____

_____

_____

_____

_____

What consistent habits or systems can you implement to make leadership development a core part of your organizational culture?

_____

_____

_____

_____

_____

ACTION WORKSHEET:
LEADERSHIP DEVELOPMENT COACHING ASSESSMENT

Developing leaders is one of the most impactful investments you can make in your organization. Use this worksheet to assess how effectively you identify, coach, and empower emerging leaders. Reflect honestly to determine where your approach builds confidence—and where it can grow stronger.

Rating Scale:
1–Rarely demonstrates this behavior   5–Consistently demonstrates this behavior

COACHING FOCUS	CURRENT REALITY	HOW I CAN STRENGTHEN THIS AREA	SELF-RATING (1–5)
Identifying Potential			
Goal Setting & Clarity			
Coaching & Feedback			
Succession & Sustainability			

Review your ratings and reflections. In the next section, you'll choose one area of focus to design a specific plan for developing and empowering leaders on your team.

ACTION WORKSHEET:
LEADERSHIP DEVELOPMENT IN ACTION

Leadership development becomes transformational when you move from identifying potential to activating it. Use this page to design one actionable plan that builds confidence, clarity, and capability in emerging leaders on your team.

FOCUS AREA

Which leadership development focus area from your assessment will you strengthen first, and why does it matter most to your organization's success?

_____

_____

_____

_____

_____

_____

DEVELOPMENT STRATEGY OR ACTION STEP

Describe one specific initiative, conversation, or program that will support the growth of emerging leaders.

_____

_____

_____

_____

_____

_____

EXPECTED OUTCOME

What measurable or observable results do you anticipate? How will this strengthen your leadership pipeline or culture?

_____

_____

_____

_____

_____

FOLLOW-UP & ACCOUNTABILITY PLAN

How will you track progress and ensure this development effort remains ongoing? Who will help you sustain it?

_____

_____

_____

_____

_____

LEADERSHIP INSIGHT

The most effective leaders grow others—not by giving answers, but by creating opportunities for discovery.

COACHING APPLICATION:
MY LEADERSHIP DEVELOPMENT BLUEPRINT

LEADERSHIP EXAMPLE: DEVELOPING LEADERS FROM WITHIN

A department head in a large nonprofit organization realized her team constantly relied on her for decisions. Though talented, her staff hesitated to lead without approval. She decided to shift her approach from directing to developing—introducing monthly "leadership labs," where each team member facilitated discussions, solved challenges, and shared lessons learned.

Over time, the group began demonstrating initiative and ownership. When one member was promoted to lead a new project, others stepped up seamlessly to fill the gap. What started as a training experiment evolved into a culture of empowerment—where leadership was no longer a title, but a shared responsibility.

What to Apply:
- Replace dependency with development—help team members find their own answers.
- Create regular opportunities for emerging leaders to practice decision-making and reflection.

 Lesson: Leadership multiplies when you stop leading alone and start leading others to lead.

Developing others is both an art and a discipline.

Transformational leaders create systems that help emerging leaders discover their strengths, clarify their purpose, and practice real responsibility.

Use this page to outline your personal approach to leadership development—turning awareness into action and mentorship into measurable growth.

COACH'S CHALLENGE

This month, delegate one leadership responsibility to an emerging leader—and coach them through it. Let them make the decisions, experience the pressure, and reflect on the outcome. Growth comes from guided ownership.

MY DEVELOPMENT PHILOSOPHY

What do I believe about leadership growth? How do I define success in developing others?

MY DEVELOPMENT STRATEGIES

What intentional steps or programs will I use to identify, mentor, and equip emerging leaders?

MY COACHING STRENGTHS

What qualities, experiences, or skills help me effectively develop leadership in others?

MY GROWTH OPPORTUNITIES

Where can I improve my ability to empower others and create sustainable leadership pipelines?

The greatest legacy of any leader is not achievement —it's the leaders they leave behind.

LIVING ON PURPOSE
Your leadership legacy is built every time you help someone else discover theirs.

LIVING ON PURPOSE PROMPT:

How are you currently investing in the growth of others?

What intentional actions can you take to develop leaders who will continue the work long after you?

_____

_____

_____

_____

_____

_____

_____

_____

_____

_____

_____

_____

_____

LIVING THE PROMISE:

Leadership development is the highest form of influence. Write a short statement describing how you will intentionally coach and empower someone this month to step into leadership.

My declaration: _____

_____

_____

_____

_____

_____

_____

_____

_____

_____

✓ CHAPTER 9: LEADERSHIP PROGRESS CHECK

☐	I reflected on how my leadership practices influence the growth and confidence of others.
☐	I identified opportunities to strengthen my organization's leadership pipeline and development culture.
☐	I implemented one intentional action to mentor or coach an emerging leader.
☐	I committed to building systems that make leadership development a continuous process, not a one-time event.

NOTES FROM COACHING CONVERSATIONS
SELF-REFLECTIONS

Adapting, Innovating, and Inspiring in a Changing World

> **FROM THE BOOK**
>
> This section expands on Transformational Leadership: Unleashing Your Full Potential — Chapter 10: "The Future of Transformational Leadership."
>
> In this chapter, Dr. Jonathan K. Jefferson challenges leaders to think beyond current practices and embrace transformation as a lifelong mindset.
> He explores how innovation, technology, global collaboration, and changing workforce dynamics are reshaping what effective leadership looks like.
>
> Use this section to envision your role in shaping the future—leading with agility, empathy, and purpose in an ever-evolving world.

The future belongs to leaders who can evolve without losing their foundation.

Transformational leadership is not static—it's a living process that grows as people, systems, and challenges change. As the world demands more collaboration and consciousness, leaders must balance innovation with integrity and progress with purpose.

Tomorrow's success will come not from authority, but from adaptability and the ability to inspire continuous transformation.

CHAPTER GOALS

- Explore how global, technological, and cultural shifts influence leadership practices.
- Identify skills and mindsets essential for leading in the future.
- Develop a personal vision for lifelong growth as a transformational leader.

WHEN TO USE

Use this section when planning for organizational change, building innovation strategies, or redefining your leadership approach for the next generation.

"The future of leadership is not about keeping up with change—it's about creating it."

— *Dr. Jonathan K. Jefferson*

REFLECTION & AWARENESS

The future of leadership will demand flexibility, creativity, and courage. Before you can lead others through change, you must reflect on how you adapt, innovate, and stay grounded in purpose. **Use the prompts below to explore how you're preparing yourself—and others—for the next era of transformational leadership.**

How comfortable are you with uncertainty and change in your leadership environment?

_____

_____

_____

_____

What practices help you stay innovative while maintaining focus on your core values and mission?

_____

_____

_____

_____

How do you use technology and collaboration to enhance your leadership impact?

_____

_____

_____

_____

What emerging trends or challenges could reshape how you lead in the next five years?

_____

_____

_____

_____

_____

How are you preparing the next generation of leaders to think critically, act ethically, and adapt quickly?

_____

_____

_____

_____

_____

What daily habits will help you continue learning, evolving, and leading with vision in a rapidly changing world?

_____

_____

_____

_____

_____

ACTION WORKSHEET:
FUTURE-READY LEADERSHIP ASSESSMENT

The future of transformational leadership depends on your ability to learn, unlearn, and adapt. Use this worksheet to assess your preparedness to lead through complexity, innovation, and change. Reflect honestly to identify where you're thriving—and where new growth is needed to stay future-ready.

Rating Scale:
1–Rarely demonstrates this behavior   5–Consistently demonstrates this behavior

LEADERSHIP FOCUS	CURRENT REALITY	HOW I CAN STRENGTHEN THIS AREA	SELF-RATING (1–5)
Adaptability & Resilience			
Innovation & Creativity			
Technology & Collaboration			
Vision & Foresight			

Review your scores and notes. In the next section, you'll choose one focus area to strengthen through a future-focused leadership initiative.

ACTION WORKSHEET:
FUTURE-READY LEADERSHIP IN ACTION

Leading the future means shaping it.

Use this page to create a focused plan for building adaptability, innovation, and vision into your leadership practice and team culture.

FOCUS AREA

Which area from your assessment will you prioritize for growth? Why is it critical to your long-term success as a leader?

LEADERSHIP INITIATIVE OR STRATEGY

Describe a specific action, project, or learning goal that will help you and your team prepare for future challenges and opportunities.

EXPECTED IMPACT

What change do you anticipate as a result—greater innovation, stronger engagement, improved resilience, or clearer vision?

_____

_____

_____

_____

_____

SUSTAINABILITY & REFLECTION PLAN

How will you maintain adaptability and keep learning as conditions evolve? What systems will help you track progress?

_____

_____

_____

_____

_____

LEADERSHIP INSIGHT

The future favors leaders who learn faster, adapt sooner, and stay anchored in purpose.

COACHING APPLICATION:
MY FUTURE LEADERSHIP BLUEPRINT

LEADERSHIP EXAMPLE: LEADING TOWARD TOMORROW

A CEO of a mid-sized tech firm noticed her leadership team struggling to keep up with emerging digital tools and shifting market demands.

Instead of pushing for immediate results, she created a "Future Fridays" initiative—one hour each week dedicated to learning something new. Team members shared brief presentations on the trends, technologies, and ideas shaping their industries.

Within a few months, participation grew beyond leadership circles. Cross-department teams began collaborating on small innovation projects that later evolved into key business solutions.

The company didn't just catch up to change—it began driving it.

What to Apply:
- Encourage learning as a daily leadership habit, not a crisis response.
- Create spaces where experimentation and curiosity are recognized as strengths.

 Lesson: Transformation thrives in cultures that value learning, not just knowing.

The future of leadership starts with vision—yours.

Transformational leaders stay ahead of change by blending innovation with authenticity and growth with grounded purpose.

Use this page to define how you'll evolve as a leader who adapts, inspires, and shapes the future with integrity.

 COACH'S TIP

The future won't wait for you to be ready —stay curious, stay teachable, and stay in motion.

MY FUTURE VISION

What kind of leader do I want to become over the next five years? How will I measure my growth and impact?

MY INNOVATION STRATEGY

What new ideas, tools, or perspectives will I explore to stay creative and adaptable in my leadership?

MY LEADERSHIP VALUES

Which core values will anchor me as I lead through change and uncertainty?

MY DEVELOPMENT PLAN

What consistent learning, reflection, or coaching practices will I commit to as part of my ongoing growth?

The future isn't waiting to be discovered—it's waiting to be designed by leaders who keep growing.

LIVING ON PURPOSE
Your purpose shapes the future when you lead with courage, curiosity, and conviction.

LIVING ON PURPOSE PROMPT:

How will you continue growing as a transformational leader in a world that's constantly changing?

What commitments will you make today to ensure your leadership evolves with purpose and impact?

LIVING THE PROMISE:

The next chapter of leadership begins with you. Write a short statement describing how you will live out transformational leadership in the years ahead—adapting, inspiring, and leading with vision.

My declaration: _____

_____

_____

_____

_____

_____

_____

_____

_____

_____

_____

☑ CHAPTER 10: LEADERSHIP PROGRESS CHECK

☐	I reflected on how emerging trends and global changes will influence my leadership approach.
☐	I identified personal and professional growth areas essential for leading into the future.
☐	I developed one actionable plan to strengthen adaptability, creativity, and innovation in my leadership.
☐	I committed to lifelong learning and continuous transformation as a guiding leadership principle.

NOTES FROM COACHING CONVERSATIONS
SELF-REFLECTIONS

_____
_____
_____
_____
_____
_____
_____
_____
_____
_____
_____
_____
_____
_____
_____
_____
_____
_____
_____

CONTINUING THE JOURNEY

A space to reflect, renew, and realign your leadership growth.

Growth occurs when reflection leads to renewal.
Let this next section remind you that leadership evolution is a continuous process — not a destination.

VISION TRACKER
ANNUAL LEADERSHIP CHECK-IN

A yearly reflection to revisit your Future Leadership Blueprint.

YEAR/DATE OF REVIEW: _____

1 Vision Progress

What aspects of your long-term leadership vision have you advanced or achieved since your last review?

....

....

....

2 Key Lessons Learned

What new insights, challenges, or opportunities have shaped your leadership this year?

....

....

....

3 Adaptations for the Year Ahead

What will you change, refine, or recommit to in the next stage of your leadership journey?

....

....

....

4 Updated Leadership Focus Word or Phrase

Choose one word or short phrase that captures your leadership focus for the upcoming year:

....

Use annually to update your Future Leadership Blueprint

> **Every transformational journey is shaped by the people who walk beside us.**

Thank you to the leaders, mentors, and readers who continue to embody the principles of growth, service, and purpose-driven leadership. Your willingness to reflect, adapt, and invest in others ensures that the work of transformation continues far beyond these pages.

This workbook was created as a practical companion to *Transformational Leadership: Unleashing Your Full Potential* to help leaders move from insight to implementation—turning belief into behavior and vision into results.

Your next steps begin here:

1. Revisit your Leadership Blueprint. Update it regularly as your leadership journey evolves.
2. Coach others. Share what you've learned with a peer, mentee, or emerging leader. Transformation grows stronger when it's shared.
3. Continue the conversation. Stay connected through future programs, leadership workshops, and coaching experiences inspired by Transformational Leadership.

"Transformation is not about becoming someone new.
It's about becoming more of who you were created to be."
— Dr. Jonathan K. Jefferson

1 The Four I's of Transformational Leadership

The foundation of every transformational leader's mindset and behavior.

DIMENSION	DEFINITION	APPLICATION EXAMPLE
Idealized Influence	Lead by example; model the behavior you expect from others.	Demonstrate integrity, consistency, and shared accountability.
Inspirational Motivation	Communicate vision with clarity and enthusiasm.	Use storytelling and vision statements to ignite purpose.
Intellectual Stimulation	Encourage creativity and challenge assumptions.	Ask open-ended questions and welcome new ideas.
Individualized Consideration	Recognize the unique potential of each team member.	Provide tailored feedback, coaching, and development opportunities.

2 The G.R.O.W. Coaching Model

A proven framework for guiding coaching conversations.

DIMENSION	DEFINITION	APPLICATION EXAMPLE
G - Goal	Clarify the desired outcome.	"What does success look like for you in this situation?"
R- Reality	Explore current circumstances and barriers.	"What's happening right now?"
O- Options	Identify possible paths forward.	"What choices do you have?"
W - Way Forward	Commit to specific actions and accountability.	"What will you do next, and by when?"

3 The Mission Alignment Framework

Connecting organizational purpose to people, processes, and performance.

Core Idea:

When an organization's mission, vision, and daily practices are aligned, energy flows toward impact—not confusion.

Leadership Actions:

- Revisit the mission regularly and make it visible in every meeting.
- Align budget and priorities with stated values.
- Use storytelling to connect daily work to a broader purpose.
- Recognize individuals and teams who embody the mission in action.

4 The Transformational Growth Cycle

A continuous rhythm of reflection, action, and renewal.

Reflect → Act → Evaluate → Refine

Use this cycle to keep growth intentional:

- **Reflect:** Assess current reality and purpose.
- **Act:** Implement one focused change.
- **Evaluate:** Review outcomes and lessons learned.
- **Refine:** Adjust and recommit to the next growth goal.

5 The Leadership Promise Framework

A personal covenant for consistency, authenticity, and purpose-driven leadership.

Core Idea:

Your Leadership Promise is a short statement that defines how you intend to show up as a leader—anchoring your behavior, values, and decisions in purpose.

How to Apply:

- Reflect on your personal values and how they guide your leadership.
- Write one clear statement beginning with "As a leader, I will…"
- Revisit it each quarter to realign your actions and renew your commitment to growth.

Example:

"As a leader, I will model integrity, lead with empathy, and empower others to discover their own potential."

YOUR JOURNEY CONTINUES

Transformation is not an event—it's a journey.

Every reflection you've written, every plan you've created,
and every action you've taken brings you closer
to leading with greater purpose, presence, and impact.

The principles in these pages are not meant to end here.
They are meant to be lived—
practiced, refined, and renewed each time
you face a new challenge or embrace a new opportunity.

Keep leading with curiosity.
Keep listening with compassion.
Keep learning with humility.

And above all—keep transforming.

Because the world doesn't just need more leaders.
It needs transformational leaders
who are willing to evolve, serve,
and inspire others to do the same.

Reflection:
What does the next stage of your transformational leadership journey look like?

— Dr. Jonathan K. Jefferson
Author of Transformational Leadership: Unleashing Your Full Potential

NOTES

www.ingramcontent.com/pod-product-compliance
Lightning Source LLC
Chambersburg PA
CBHW041427120626

46547CB00002B/118